The Bramanville Girls

A memoir of six close friends from Millbury,
Massachusetts who found a unique way to
entertain servicemen during World War II.
Their light-hearted and adventurous romp
throughout the war will leave you laughing and
applauding their generosity and ingenuity.

Beverly McLean Cambridge

authorHOUSE®

AuthorHouse™
1663 Liberty Drive
Bloomington, IN 47403
www.authorhouse.com
Phone: 1-800-839-8640

First published by AuthorHouse 11/05/2010

ISBN: 978-1-4520-6505-2 (e)
ISBN: 978-1-4520-6504-5 (sc)
ISBN: 978-1-4520-6503-8 (hc)

Library of Congress Control Number: 2010912201

Printed in the United States of America

This book is printed on acid-free paper.

Dedication

This book is dedicated to Shirley Brodin who was my closest friend right up to her final days. I miss her deeply and after writing this memoir I realized she was perhaps the most vibrant and entertaining of all the girls. Because of her unending curiosity, I always felt she would have made a wonderful CIA agent!

It is also dedicated to all of our wonderful mothers who not only supported us in our endeavors, but provided most of the wonderful food we fed to the servicemen.

Acknowledgements

I would like to express my sincere thanks to Marian MacPhail and Nancy and Bill Davis who were kind enough to take the time to edit my manuscript.

Also, I would like to thank Sue Tagliareni for all of my interruptions during her business day in Boston. She calmed me down when I thought I had lost the manuscript in my computer and helped me to understand so many functions that were new to me in the age of technology.

Finally, I would never have had the patience to finish this book if it had not been for Janet Stein. When I was in trouble, she would drive an hour or so to Hampton, New Hampshire from Boston, Massachusetts after her long hours at work and would cheerfully spend an hour or two or three helping me to get back on track. When I was ready to throw in the towel she would convince me that my efforts were not in vain and I would be rewarded when I finally saw my book in print. I will be forever indebted to her for all of her help and encouragement and for all she taught me in the process.

Awakening early, I watched a breathtaking sunrise from the balcony of our cliff-side hotel in Dubrovnik overlooking the sparkling Adriatic Sea. My husband was still asleep and I wanted to wake him to share this moment with me since it was the last day of our two-week trip through Austria and Yugoslavia. He had not been feeling well most of the ten days we had been traveling, so I decided to let him sleep as long as he could. He had been hospitalized in the Spring with what the doctors thought was a chemical pneumonia, but as the Fall approached and our trip drew nearer, I noticed he was losing weight. I begged him to see the doctor again. He was told his white blood count was low, but the doctor felt a vacation would be good for him and said to see him when he returned. As our trip progressed I could see that he was losing more weight and not eating very much. At each major city, I wanted to make reservations to return home immediately, but he kept insisting that we go on.

I dressed and went down to the dining room for breakfast and then decided I would go for my last swim as we were leaving for London the next day and then back to the states the following day. The beaches in Yugoslavia were mostly black rock rather than sand, especially this far south, so I tiptoed gingerly into the icy but refreshing water and swam for ten minutes or so. As I was walking out of the ocean I felt something sharp beneath my right foot. I reached down to pick it up, thinking it was just a jagged rock. It was difficult to determine what it was because it was covered with rust, but I decided it was a dog tag with the chain still attached. The name and ID numbers were not legible due to the rust. I put on my beach robe and placed the dog tag in my pocket. I walked slowly back to the hotel to locate the concierge. I asked him if he could find something to clean the dog tag and he said he would try. As I waited anxiously for him to return, I kept telling myself that there were probably hundreds of dog tags from WWII lying on the ocean bottoms throughout Europe. After what seemed to be an eternity, the concierge returned and handed me the dog tag. Enough letters were now legible enough for me to see that it was the dog tag of Bernard F. Devoe and I stared and stared at them in disbelief. I must have turned very pale because the concierge said, "Madam, would you like a glass of water?" I told him I was fine and probably had too much sun.

I don't know how long I sat there on the large stone deck, staring at the object in my hand. It just wasn't possible, I told myself, as I fondled the dog tag. But deep down I knew it was Dev's dog tag because I also recognized some of the serial numbers on the chain.

I didn't want to return to our room just yet, so I stayed in the comfortable chaise lounge overlooking the beach. I lay there for a long time as cold shivers ran through my body, trying to comprehend why, on this day and in this place, a simple swim in the ocean would reopen a chapter of my life that had closed thirty years ago. I tried hard to get it out of my mind, but could not keep my thoughts from turning back thirty-three long years to the summer of 1940 and the events of the next five years which would affect our lives in so many ways.

Contents

Millbury, Massachusetts

The summer of 1940 was approaching as I finished my junior year in Millbury High School and I was eagerly looking forward to my summer vacation with five close friends.

Millbury was a thriving mill town in the Blackstone Valley of Massachusetts, just six miles south of Worcester. It was known primarily for its cotton and woolen mills, but there were many other industries such as linen thread, felt and small tools, all of which played an important role when we entered World War II. The many ponds and lakes in town were very important to these industries as they supplied the electric power necessary for the operation of their mills.

I lived just west of the center of town in a section called Bramanville, and my father worked for the Linen Thread Co. as a maintenance engineer. We lived in duplex mill houses across from the mill and like my father, most of the men came over from Northern Ireland to work in this mill.

Our complex was on a busy street, surrounded by water on three sides, and on a summer evening you could hear music blaring forth from the player pianos in most of the houses. Thus our cluster of homes became known as "Musical Island".

While life went on as usual for us in the U.S., things were going from bad to worse in Europe. England had already entered the war with Germany in 1939 and Hitler invaded Poland in 1940. France fell in 1940, but President Franklin D. Roosevelt was determined to keep us out of it so we didn't pay too much attention to the daily news on the radio at that time.

The Bramanville Girls

Shirley Brodin

Shirl and I first met in the third grade of Burbank School. She was a tall, beautiful brunette of Swedish and French extraction. She had a natural comic flair born of her appealing naivety and was very popular with boys and girls alike. She lived on Burbank Hill, close to the grade school we both attended.

Florence Horne

Flo was a close friend of Shirl's who also lived on Burbank Hill. Flo was a stunning brunette, very tall and two years younger than Shirl and me. Flo's father and grandfather both worked in Horne's General Store in Bramanville. Everyone shopped there for groceries and other sundries since there were no supermarkets yet in the town.

Margaret Hogan

Margaret, a very pretty Irish lass, was also my classmate and was more serious than the rest of us, sometimes finding it difficult to go along with some of our crazy pranks. She was very intelligent and kept us up on current events, especially when we entered the war in Europe on December 7, 1941, after the Japanese bombed Pearl Harbor in Hawaii. The rest of us were more interested in the "home front" and how we would survive when the boys all went off to war.

Elva Stevens

Steve was a ravishing redhead who was the most unflappable person I have ever known. Nothing fazed her and she had a very dry sense of humor. Her folks had a lovely summer home on Lake Singletary and we always had their Old Town canoe and sailboat at our disposal. Elva was a wonderful sailor and we all quickly learned how to paddle a canoe.

Beverly McLean

I was a tall platinum blond who perhaps was the most daring and adventurous of the group due to my vivid imagination. I never considered myself beautiful, but I guess I was attractive in some ways (I hated my full head of natural wavy hair which the boys used to tease me about. It wasn't until I later went to work in Worcester that I realized there was such a thing as a hair "stylist" who did a much better job than the local barber in cutting my hair!) I had a good sense of humor and a penchant for cleanliness that exists to this day. As an Aries, I was a true pioneer, always ready for a new adventure.

Phyllis Lacouture

Phyl was the last to join our group. She had gone to a parochial school and entered my freshman class of high school in 1938 but we never became close friends until the summer of 1940. Her mother opened an ice cream parlor in a small empty building in front of their home on Brierley's Pond in Bramanville. It soon became a popular spot for everyone in town and also people coming from Worcester who had to pass by on their way to their summer homes on Lake Singletary and Ramshorn Pond. Phyl and her younger sister and brother all worked in the store, but we found it difficult to get to know Phyl who was very shy and never seemed to be in the store when we visited. She later told us she used to hide in the back room when she saw us coming, but deep down she longed to be one of us. She had a terrific personality and a contagious laugh which we soon discovered when we got to know her better.

Lake Singletary And The Horne Brothers

Flo's great grandfather, William E. Horne, opened Horne's General Store many years before we were all born, but I remember Grandma Horne clearly from my younger days when you always got a penny's worth of candy when you came in to pay your bill!

Wally was the youngest of the five sons who worked in the store and in the early 1930's he built a camp on Lake Singletary, a beautiful six mile long body of water bordering the towns of Millbury and Sutton. When the devastating 1938 hurricane wiped out all of the Rhode Island shoreline, it also came inland as far as Worcester, doing considerable damage in all the surrounding towns. One of its targets was a large tree that fell on the camp, but fortunately didn't crash through, leaving only a swayback roof.

Unfortunately, Wally died very young, before the camp was completely finished and the whole town mourned his premature passing. He left a widow and three children who all went to live with an aunt in Rhode Island.

No one ever used the camp after Wally died. Occasionally we would stop by to have a swim or just sit outside on the stone wall in front of the camp. As the close of school approached in the summer of 1940, we thought it would be great if we could get permission to spend our entire summer vacation there. There were four bedrooms, a small kitchen with a kerosene stove, an icebox, and a hand pump in the sink to get water. There was a large living/dining room in the center of the camp with a brick fireplace at one end. In front of the living room was another large room which obviously was intended as a porch since it had many windows facing the lake. Two large sofas and many wicker chairs made it very comfy looking. To our delight, there was a large Victrola on a small table on the porch.

There was no indoor plumbing, but we loved the novelty of the "outhouse" in back of the cottage which was covered by a grape arbor. We could grab a bunch of grapes on the way in and to this day I have never had sweeter, plumper or more delicious grapes than those blue Concords. There were a few magazines and books on a small shelf, and I'm sure it is the only place we did any reading at all that summer!

The Chaperone

The Horne brothers all agreed we could use the cottage for the summer provided we had a chaperone. We had only one person in mind – Sadie Russell – who was a close friend of my family and about ten years older than me. Like my father, her family had all come over from Ireland and her father and an aunt were also employed by the Linen Thread Mill. I had known Sadie all my life and the other girls had come to know her as well, so she was a unanimous choice. She was a beautiful woman with a wonderful sense of humor who was constantly smiling or laughing. She had nicknamed us "Les Girls" and thoroughly enjoyed the crazy things we did. She readily agreed to be our "chaperone" and so we prepared to move in bag and baggage the minute school closed in June.

Phyl Joins The Bramanville Girls

The night before we moved in, we were all at Flo's home for supper and her mother, Susie, said "Why don't you invite that nice girl in the store on Brierley's to join you at the camp?" We were surprised to hear that because we hardly knew her, but gave it serious thought. We had enough room for another person since there were four bedrooms. We knew she could cook and we were badly in need of a good cook, so off we went to find her. As usual, she was nowhere to be seen, but we told her mother we would like to speak to her. She went into the back room to get Phyl, who came out very slowly and shyly. No sooner had we extended the invitation when she ran out the door to their home behind the store, packed a bag and was ready to join us the next morning!

Moving Day

Two days after school ended, we happily moved into the camp with the strains of the "Hut Sut" song blasting forth from the old Victrola on the porch.

We gave the camp a good hosing inside (the knotholes in the floor were large enough for the water to escape), threw the mattresses into the lake to get rid of the musty smell (a bad mistake we learned later), picked up a chunk of ice at Horne's ice house nearby, and finally sat down to take it all in because we still couldn't believe our dream had come true!

We drew names to see who would be roommates. Shirl and Margaret shared a bedroom, Phyl and Flo, and Sadie and me while she was our chaperone. Elva would sleep at her folks' cottage while Sadie was with us. Later, when our folks felt we didn't need one anymore, Elva and I became roommates. That left us with a spare room which we used as our "coffee salon" where we would have our after-dinner coffee and our daily cigarette. None of us inhaled so the camp would smell like an incinerator and we quickly had to get rid of the smoke before any of our folks arrived for a visit at night. Besides being known as The Bramanville Girls, we were also known in town as The Debs. We were never sure why, but we were taller than most girls our age, and because we were such a close-knit group, were perhaps thought of as somewhat snobbish. One of the tobacco manufacturers came out with a cigarette brand called "The Debs" which had red tip filters, so naturally they became our favorite cigarette!

We loved our Coffee Salon which we used every night, and I remember one day an Army truck pulled into our driveway with some of the soldiers we had met from Ft. Devens at a USO dance there. They could only stay for a few hours, but they wanted to bring us a present - a 50 gallon drum of precious gasoline! We, of course, were thrilled and they carried it into the camp and asked us where we wanted to keep it. We told them to put it in our Coffee Salon and we immediately covered it with a tablecloth so no one would ask us where we got it. We put a couple of ashtrays on the barrel and couldn't believe our good fortune.

One night Flo's father, Ralph, stopped by with a few groceries as we were having our coffee and cigarette and he noticed the new piece of furniture. Since we had to douse our cigarettes in a hurry when his car pulled in, we neglected to remove the ashtrays from the barrel. He wanted to know what was in the barrel and when we told him, he went ballistic. "My God", he said, "if you girls are smoking in this room, don't you realize you could blow yourselves and the camp to bits?!!" He went back to the store and returned with his delivery truck and removed the barrel from our premises. We never dared to ask him what became of it and we mourned its loss as it was worth $75.00 or more.

I don't think we spent very much on groceries, relying on our folks to furnish most of our food. We would often call upon them to prepare a casserole or dessert for our supper and would make the rounds late in the afternoon to pick these up. I do remember that our little icebox wasn't exactly bulging with food, but we never seemed to be hungry so I guess we ate enough to survive our active days!

The 1927 LaSalle

We were now happily ensconced in our new summer home, but we decided we were missing one important thing.... transportation. I had turned 16 on March 24th and went to the DMV that very day to get my driver's license. We all had family cars and could use them on special occasions, but we now realized we were stranded on Singletary since the bus from Worcester only made infrequent runs from Bramanville to Singletary Nook. Flo's grandfather, Arthur Ithemar Horne (A.I. to everyone and Pa to all of us), owned a 1927 LaSalle sedan which looked like one of the getaway cars that the Chicago gangsters used during the Prohibition. All paint was gone so it had a rusty look, and tires so badly worn in places you could see canvas where rubber had been. It had curtains in all the back windows, a windshield that could be raised to let more air in, plus a cigarette lighter that could reach into the back seat. Pa only used the car occasionally to go to a movie in Worcester, so it was idle all day while he worked in the store. Flo agreed to ask his permission to use it when it was idle, and because he was such a wonderful grandfather to all of us and adored Flo, he readily agreed. To say we were floating on Cloud 9 is putting it mildly. We picked up the car that very night and although we were restricted to local driving within a radius of ten miles, this allowed us to go as far as Worcester where we could get gas for fifteen cents a gallon at a Merit Gas Station. Pa had filled the tank for us, but it didn't take us long to empty it since we only got 9 miles to a gallon. When we needed gas, we would drive by Dolan's News Stand in Millbury Center where there were always a few boys hanging about. We would fill the car (sometimes we could squeeze 10 people in) and off we would go to the Merit Station for a dollar's worth of gas. All passengers had to chip in ten cents apiece, and we were there so often the owner pumping the gas would just count the number of people in the car and fill the tank accordingly!

It had a large, flat steering wheel that was similar to that on a bus. If we came to a really sharp corner, the person sitting next to me had to help turn the wheel since there was no power steering in those days. It had a long shift that was easy to operate and a hand brake that became essential because in time the foot brake didn't work at all and I had to rely only on the hand brake. I had some hairy experiences with that hand brake.

Since I lived on Brierley's Pond, I would sometimes take

the Ark home to wash and polish it. Sadie, who lived next door to me, said she used to feel sorry for me for trying to make it shine since there was no paint left on the car. But I couldn't have loved it more if it had been a modern Rolls Royce. When I bought my first car it was a light green 1936 LaSalle convertible with a rumble seat and yellow sidewall tires which were a rarity. Although I loved that car, nothing could take the place of that 1927 LaSalle.

Naming The Camp And The Lasalle

So now we had our own summer home and our own car and we decided to name them. It didn't take long to come up with names, especially for the LaSalle which resembled an ark! (Like Noah's Ark there was no limit to the number of people we could squeeze into it!) So we christened it the "Ark" with a bottle of Coke, and it became known all around town, although some folks preferred to call it the Black Maria.

THE ARK

Naming the camp took longer, but one day we were sitting in the shade behind the cottage and someone had put the Hut Sut record on the Victrola. There were a lot of people from Quinsigamond Village who had camps on the lake and we soon became very friendly with several of the boys our age. Suddenly it occurred to me: "Let's name the camp the "Hut Sut!" The Hut Sut was a popular song that year and the lyrics went something like this: "The Ralson is a Swedish town, the Rillera is a stream, the Brawla is the boy and girl, and the Hut Sut is their dream...." Surely it was our dream come true and everyone agreed it was a wonderful name for our summer home.

THE HUT SUT

Pa stopped by that evening for a brief visit (always with lots of groceries from the store), and we told him we had a name for the camp. He went right home to his workshop and the next day he brought us the wonderful sign he had made.

We were ecstatic as he nailed it to the back wall of the camp for all to see as they entered our humble abode!

The Working Girl

Phyl was the only one who had a summer job that year. She worked at the public library in Millbury Center and we would drive down to pick her up at noon and then return her to the library at 1:00 p.m. If we were having something hot for lunch (mostly leftovers, especially a dish she made from leftover corn, onions, and potatoes which I still often make), then we had to start the kerosene stove at 10:00 a.m. so it would be hot by twelve. We had some pretty hot and humid days during that summer and Phyl minded the heat more than the rest of us. So there she stood over that hot stove with perspiration pouring down her cheeks while we sat patiently waiting for lunch to be ready! She had no time to cool off before we had to rush her back to the library, while we returned to the camp for a cool swim in the lake. I shudder now to think how cruel that was!

Phyl was also the only who had a "steady" boyfriend at that time, a very nice fellow from Sutton, a neighboring town. Because of that and the fact that she wore eyeshadow and eyelash makeup, we felt she was a little too "fast" for us. But we really liked her and, of course, she was a great cook, so we decided we could overlook those shortcomings. Besides, we loved to peek out our bedroom windows to watch them kissing when they parked in the driveway after returning from their night out.

We also went through her bureau drawer and applied some of her makeup, but we never looked as good as she did!

The Millbury Boys

BACK ROW: RAY, BUSTER, DEV, JOE, JOE
MIDDLE ROW: FLO, MARGARET, JOHNNY, WALTER, FRANCIS, ELVA
FRONT ROW: SHIRL, PHYL, BEV

None of us had "steady" boyfriends at that time, but there was a "gang" of Millbury boys we spent most of our time with year round. In the winter, we would have a party every Sunday night on Flo's large enclosed front porch where we could dance and play our favorite games. We would collect a quarter from each boy to buy snacks and cokes. In the summer they would come up to the camp to spend the evening with us. They always complained that we never had enough snacks so we told them to bring their own, along with Cokes! Flo's mother, Susie, loaned us a small melodeon and we would sing the night away from my popular sheet music and old song books. Shirl and I both played the piano, but I always seemed to be the one who did the honors. We would also play records on the Victrola and dance to some of the popular songs of the Big Bands – Glenn Miller, Tommy Dorsey, Benny Goodman, Woody Herman, to name a few. Because noise carries further over water, some of our neighbors often complained about the constant ruckus emanating from our camp. At one point, they started a petition to bar us from the lake, but thankfully they never succeeded in getting rid of us!

My brother Ray was one of the "gang" and there was Bernard Devoe, Buster Ethier, Maurice O'Brien, Walter Weldon, Joe Goryl, Francis Hamilton, Johnny Hamilton, and Bob (Pepe) Ducharme.

The Millbury boys thought of us as theirs alone, so they were not too happy when they discovered we were entertaining other groups of boys at the Hut Sut. Although they were stretching their wings, they didn't take kindly to us stretching ours. But once we had transportation, there was no end to our discoveries and conquests!

Bernard Devoe

Dev (pronounced Deev) was a tall, handsome blond and I did have a terrific crush on him. It started one day in the 8th grade when the teacher called on him to critique a wild story I had written. He said wonderful things about it - original, imaginative, etc. - and it was love at first word. From that day on and all through high school, I couldn't be interested in any other boy. But the other girls and boys teased him about me which turned him against me for a while. But as we continued to see each other when the "gang" got together and as we all matured, the teasing stopped and we became good friends.

He and Shirley both worked after school at Dolan's Newsstand in the center of town and they occasionally dated. I of course was envious, but never let her know because we were such good friends. I would have loved to have gone out with him, but was careful not to let him know how I still felt about him. I was happy to just be in the same room with him, singing together and occasionally dancing with him.

SHIRL, DEV, BEV, BOB, PHYL

Our Favorite Evening Jaunts

If the Millbury boys didn't drop in for an evening of fun, we would pile into the Ark and take a ride to Worcester to make the rounds of all the colleges – Holy Cross, Clark University and Worcester Polytechnic Institute. Harrington Corner in downtown Worcester was a favorite hangout of the college boys and as we rattled past in the Ark, leaning heavily on the horn (as if we needed that to get their attention!), a huge cheer would go up from the crowd! We, of course, thought the cheers were for us, but I'm sure it was the Ark they were acknowledging!

Another favorite route was to Whitinsville, which was about 7 miles south of Millbury. We were all enamored with some of the basketball and football stars from that town, especially one quarterback who warranted many "Hubba Hubba's" each time we saw him. Hubba Hubba was an expression at that time that translated to "Wow, isn't he cute?" Whenever we could get close enough, we would snap his picture on Flo's Kodak box camera and get a thrill just looking at those snapshots over and over again. I don't think he even knew we existed. We would often go to pre-football game dances on a Friday night at the Whitins Gym and would sit in the balcony, hoping our heartthrob might ask one of us to dance. Of course he never did, but it was exciting just seeing him dance with others.

Fitton Field, Holy Cross College

We went to many of the football games at Fitton Field in Worcester as we knew some of the fellows who played on the Holy Cross team. There was a large parking lot next to the stadium and we always created a stir when we arrived in the Ark.

One day we arrived quite early and as we rode by the stadium, I noticed a road that ran under some of the bleachers. Without giving it a thought, I turned the car onto the road and suddenly we were circling the field. A roar went up from the crowd so I went around three or four times until we heard some sirens blasting and onto the field came the Holy Cross police! They stopped us and asked what we thought we were doing, and we had to make up a fast excuse. We told them we thought it was the road to the parking lot which they didn't buy, but they let us go and said if we ever did it again, we would all be arrested!

We were thrilled when we were written up in the Holy Cross newspaper! We loved free publicity and would gladly have furnished a picture of all of us in the Ark had we known we were going to make headlines!

Needless to say, we never tried it again!

Millbury Is Invaded

We were coming home from school one day in late May of 1941 and as we approached Elmwood Street where Elva and Margaret lived, we were amazed to find camouflaged soldiers all over the roadside and nearby fields. Since we had not yet entered the war in Europe, we had no idea what they were doing in our hometown. It didn't take us long to become acquainted with some of them, and we learned they were on summer maneuvers from Fort Devens in Ayer, MA. As you can imagine, this was the most exciting thing that had happened in our young lives. We couldn't wait for school to end each day so we could rush to Elmwood Street to continue our rendezvous with the invading Army!

When the maneuvers ended in two weeks, we were quite bored and downhearted until we received a call from one of the soldiers we had met. He and a friend wanted to come to Millbury to visit us. We said we would be delighted to see them, but could he bring four more fellows since there were six of us. He said he was sure he could, and so we made plans to meet them in Worcester the following

Saturday afternoon. He said they would like to bring steaks and all the trimmings and they would be happy to cook dinner for us. What a treat, especially for Phyl!

Our mothers weren't too happy when they heard our plans. Up until now they knew we were safe in the hands of the Millbury boys, but they agreed to the arrangements we had made. As always, Flo's home was the ideal spot for our rendezvous since her folks usually were out when they weren't entertaining at home on Saturday night.

So off we went late Saturday afternoon to pick up the soldiers, and sure enough there were six of them. We knew it would be better for only two of us to pick them up, but no one wanted to stay behind so we all piled into the Ark. It was a jolly jaunt back to Millbury with twelve of us squeezed into the car!

While they were busy in the kitchen unpacking the groceries and preparing to cook the dinner, Shirl decided we should go upstairs to Flo's bedroom where we had placed their jackets and go through their pockets. We questioned why this was necessary, and as usual, ever suspicious, she convinced us that we really didn't know them and who knows if they had an ulterior motive? So the search began for an "ulterior motive", even though we didn't really know what we were looking for. We found chewing gum, packs of cigarettes, some money, and other sundry items. Then in each jacket we found a small packet with several items that looked like deflated balloons. Shirl was the first to open the packet and gingerly removed one of the contents. Phyl said, "Why would they be carrying balloons?" and Shirl replied, "Maybe they plan to decorate the kitchen before they serve dinner!"

Finally it occurred to us to read the instructions on the packet and we were in utter shock! Shirl gasped: "I told you there was something suspicious about them. They are planning to rape all of us after dinner!"

We talked it over (although we weren't entirely sure what "rape" was, until Shirl of all people gave us a weird explanation), and quickly decided they had to leave without dinner. So we descended the stairs with jackets in hand and informed them that something had come up and they had to leave immediately. The steaks were in the broiler and the veggies were steaming away on the stove when Flo bravely declared "I'm sorry fellas, but you've all got to leave this house immediately."

Flabbergasted, one of the fellows said, "You want us to leave? What have we done?" Margaret said, "We would rather not discuss it. Here are your jackets. We'll drive you back to Worcester." Another one said, "Can't we eat dinner first?" And in unison we said, "No, you must leave now!"

Again, we all squeezed into the Ark, as the other girls feared if I went alone, I might be raped on the way. Safety in numbers! It was probably the fastest (I pushed the Ark to 35 miles per hour) and most silent ride in the history of a crammed car. We dropped them off at the bus station and said our goodbyes. Needless to say, we never heard from them again, and I'm sure they wondered for a long time what awful thing they had done to be treated so badly. It wasn't until a couple of years later that we learned (probably from one of the Millbury boys) that condoms were G.I. issue to all military personnel! (We will feel vindicated if one of those sorry G.I.'s ever gets to read this book.)

Shirley's Pregnancy

One summer night in 1941 when the Millbury boys were visiting us at the camp, my brother (who was a big tease) grabbed Shirley and literally dragged her into her bedroom. He threw her on the bed and gave her a passionate kiss. She was screaming so he quickly released his hold and she came running out of the bedroom. We tried scolding him but it was futile as all the other boys were in hysterics.

When they left, we sat down to console Shirley who was really more than upset. Even though most of us were 17 at the time, we knew absolutely nothing about sex, as it wasn't taught in school in those days. Our mothers told us very little, although we knew the stork didn't bring babies. But we didn't have a clue about how conception took place.

But as usual, Shirley had some inkling of it, and convinced us that she knew it took place in a bedroom. We, of course, bought this idea as we had no others to offer. She now was sure that the passionate kiss my brother had planted on her lips was the key to becoming pregnant. There was dead silence for many minutes and when she started to cry inconsolably, we tried our best to comfort her. I told her I would speak to my brother and would tell him he had to marry her. She screamed that she didn't want to marry my brother, and what was she going to tell her mother? We finally decided we would all stay at the camp until the baby arrived. Again, we weren't sure when that would be, but someone said they thought it was five or six months. We would buy her some loose-fitting clothes so it wouldn't be noticeable that she was putting on weight.

So every week for the rest of the summer we measured her waist. As the weeks went by, she seemed to be losing weight rather than gaining it. She was hardly eating a thing, so we finally decided she wasn't pregnant after all. It was quite a relief for all of us, especially Shirley, but now we still didn't know how a baby was conceived!

Farewell Millbury High School

Shirl, Phyl, Margaret and I graduated from high school in June of 1941 and it was a very sad day for me. I loved every minute of my high school days and knew it would never be quite the same again.

Phyl entered Clark University and Shirl went to a business school in Worcester. My folks could not afford college and there were not many scholarships available in those days. I was valedictorian of my class and in later years would have gotten a scholarship, so I resigned myself to entering the work force. I got a job at The Paul Revere Life Insurance Co. in Worcester and worked there until I married in 1950. Margaret also got an office job at a local company in Millbury.

Elva was in her senior year of high school and Flo was a junior, but we still managed to do many things together and spent all of our summer weekends at the Hut Sut, still entertaining the Millbury boys when they came home on leave, the sailors from WPI, and other servicemen we met after leaving high school.

The Whitinsville Boys

One evening in the Fall of 1941, we decided to take a ride to Grafton, a nearby town, where there was a Howard Johnson's Restaurant. They offered more variety in food than Donovan's and Crepeau's ice cream parlors in town, especially fried clams, and it was a pretty twenty-minute ride over back roads. There were beautiful old Colonial homes all along the Main Street and surrounding the Common, which had a lovely bandstand in the center. It became famous in the Thirties when Thornton Wilder's "Our Town" was filmed there.

When we came out of the restaurant, we noticed three attractive fellows in the car parked next to us. We exchanged smiles and then asked for their help. The right front door of the Ark sometimes came "unhinged" and I eventually learned how to quickly fix it. We found it was an excellent way to get to meet boys, as it was just as easy for me to "unhinge" it as it was to fix it. So I quickly went to work and we then asked the fellows if they could help us with a door that wasn't working properly. They eagerly offered to help and quickly fixed it. We then introduced ourselves and invited them to join us back at Flo's home. Ray attended Worcester Tech and Ken was at Northeastern in Boston. I believe Charlie was out of school, but he owned a new hydromatic Oldsmobile that was their means of transportation – much classier than ours! They were all handsome and very personable, and we were thrilled when they asked for our phone numbers and said they would like to see us again and would call to set a date.

I had a birthday coming up, and my Mother was planning a party for me, so we decided to invite Ray, Ken and Charlie and asked if they could bring three more fellows. They immediately accepted and arrived with a lovely gift of Evening in Paris, which was a popular cosmetics gift in those days. We danced and had refreshments and I could feel myself falling in love with Ray, even though Margaret had told me he had a girlfriend in Whitinsville (her brother lived there and Ray was her brother's paperboy).

Elva and I continued to date Ray and Ken throughout the winter of 1941 and into the summer of '42. Ray worked a night shift at Heald's in Worcester during his summer vacation and only had one day off. I so looked forward to those infrequent dates and I think Elva did too. They would arrange picnics at Wallum Lake in Douglas, MA and would bring all the food and soft drinks. At the end of the evening, Ray and Ken would drive Elva and me home and we would "park" on a dark road on the way to Elva's summer home. I don't know what caused it, as it only happened with Ray, but the next morning, I would notice a bruised spot on my lower lip which turned black and blue. I tried to hide it with lipstick, but it didn't always work and of course I was teased mercilessly about it. I didn't care – I was in love – and I'd be damned if I would stop kissing him!

It was a wonderful winter and summer, looking forward to seeing Ray, but it all came to an end for me after one evening at Elva's home on the lake. Her folks were out and her mother had made a wonderful casserole and some of her famous "sticky buns". I felt something was wrong, but it wasn't until they dropped me off and Ray said goodnight at the door that I realized I probably wouldn't see him anymore. Just a gut feeling, but I was right. I was devastated for a while, but of course got over it because I had always known he had a girlfriend in Whitinsville.

A Day That Will Go Down In Infamy

We were gathered at Flo's late one Sunday afternoon in early December of 1941 as her mother had invited us for supper. We were sitting in the living room with the radio on and suddenly the program we were listening to was interrupted with starting news: The Japanese had just bombed Pearl Harbor!! We were stunned, as was every American, and the next day, December 8, President Roosevelt came on the radio and declared war on the government of Japan. There were Japanese statesmen visiting in Washington when all of this happened which was hard to believe.

It was a devastating attack at 8 o'clock on a Sunday morning without any warning and caught most servicemen either still sleeping or having breakfast. The planes sneaked in through the KoleKole Pass and it wasn't until they flew over the Schofield Barracks and Hickam Air Base and started dropping bombs did anyone realize what was happening. Several battleships were destroyed at Pearl Harbor, but several other big carriers were able to leave the harbor under their own power. Our carriers had left Pearl on a resupply mission and missed the Japanese attack. Most of the planes at Hickam Field were destroyed. They had conveniently (for the Japanese) been lined up in rows out on the runways so they could be protected easier from sabotage. But it left them open to surprise bombing and strafing – hence their almost complete destruction. Two thousand servicemen and civilians were killed in these deadly attacks and many sailors were trapped beneath the Arizona. My husband and I made a point of visiting it on our first trip to Hawaii in 1971, and it was a sobering and eerie feeling to know you were standing on the gravesite of so many sailors who lost their lives that day.

The Millbury boys were coming up to Flo's that evening and we thought they would be entering service right away. But most of them didn't enlist until late in 1942 so we had another ten months of their company before they went off to war.

The Fateful Jaunt To Fort Devens

On Easter Sunday in 1942 we gathered after church in our finest clothes and decided we looked too good to not be admired! We always had a new outfit for Easter Sunday and you always wore a hat to church and gloves as well. We shed our hats and gloves and boldly decided we would drive to Fort Devens to see some of our new friends there. This was a daring adventure since we were restricted to a 10 mile radius of Millbury, but we decided to take a chance. We prayed all the way to Devens that we wouldn't have a flat tire. The last one we had was on the road coming back from Howard Johnson's in Grafton, and when the right rear tire blew, there was so much dirt inside it that it created a smoke screen around the Ark. Some boys were following us and they passed right by us and had to turn around and come back when they realized something must have happened. Our spare wasn't much better than the one that blew, but it got us home. They used our hand jack to jack up the car, and from that day on, the Ark had a tilt to the right side as they apparently jacked it up too high and it never recovered!

After stopping to primp by the side of the road, we proceeded to Devens and happily arrived at the Main Gate. All of the G.I.'s in the guard house came out to examine the car and not its passengers which really angered us. After many wisecracks about the Ark, they finally gave us a pass to enter the grounds, as many cars were backed up behind us. I put the car in gear, let out the clutch and we didn't move. I thought it was odd that the car didn't stall, and Shirley said she had seen a movie recently where some kind of "eye" kept cars from moving and stalling. So we yelled to the guards to turn off their "eye" so we could proceed. This of course brought them all out of the guard house again and we exchanged quite a few nasty words. One of them told me to get out and he would move the car out of the way. Of course the same thing happened – it didn't move, but it didn't stall either. Finally he told us we were in big trouble as we had a broken axle. Needless to say, we had no idea what an axle was, and they threw up their hands. They pushed the car to the side of the entrance while we debated what to do. We didn't dare call Pa since we weren't supposed to be so far from home. We finally decided to call Flo's father Ralph, who seemed to take our exploits in stride. This time he had to leave a dinner party at a friend's home to come to our rescue. He wasn't in a very good mood when he arrived with a heavy tow rope which he attached to our front bumper and his rear one. He drove a fairly new Buick which was much lower and lighter than the Ark, but off we went with a big sendoff from the guard house!

I was a little nervous steering since every time Ralph stopped at a traffic light I had to apply the hand brake and pray I wouldn't smash into him. When he proceeded after the light, the Buick would lift up from the road, so Ralph finally decided that the girls should all ride in the Buick, which would give it more weight. So there I was alone in the Ark, wondering if I would kill them all if the hand brake failed to work!

I stayed clear of Horne's store for quite a while after that incident, while poor Pa combed the junk yards of New England, looking for an axle that would fit the Ark. One day I had to go to the store for my Mother and as soon as I entered, Pa yelled down to one of his brothers, "Bill, guess how many miles it is to Worcester?" Bill replied, "why are you asking me that stupid question - you know it's seven miles!" Pa just smiled at me as I rushed out the door. That was the first time we realized he used to check the odometer occasionally.

So we were without wheels for a few weeks, but miraculously Pa did find a new axle and we were back in business. But from then on, we stayed within the ten mile radius and never broke the curfew again!

Falmouth Heights

In the summer of 1942, we decided we would like to spend a week on Cape Cod. One of us had heard about a place in Falmouth Heights called the Oak Crest Inn. Some relatives had stayed there and said the rooms were nice and the food was wonderful, all for $35.00 per person per week, all meals included!

We knew we couldn't use the Ark to go that far, so we asked a classmate from East Millbury named Margie Banks if she would like to join us. Margie was thrilled and said she would see if she could get her father's car for the weekend. She was not staying for the week, but said she would come back the following weekend to take us all home. He had a new Oldsmobile hydromatic, the first automatic shift made by a car manufacturer. He agreed and Margie picked us up in Bramanville around 12:30am on Saturday morning since there was a curfew on and you couldn't travel before midnight without being stopped by the police.

Three hours later we wearily arrived at the Inn and had

to waken the night desk clerk to let us in. He told us to be very quiet as guests were sleeping, so we tiptoed up to our three adjoining rooms on the second floor.

The Inn was perched on a high bluff overlooking the ocean and had a large porch which encircled the building. We were very pleased with our choice and knew we were in for an exciting week. We had been given permission by our parents to attend the dances at the USO, but were instructed not to take cigarettes from the G.I.'s, and by no means should we kiss them. If they had known we were now drinking, that would have been taboo as well!

When we went down to the dining room the next morning for a late breakfast, we could hear some of the ladies whispering, "Those are the girls who arrived in the middle of the night!" But we were determined not to let this bother us, since we would be out most of the time, and the food was great.

We spent the day on the beach at Falmouth Heights so we could go back to the Inn for lunch and then return to the beach. There was a lot of activity on the ocean at the beach, and we learned that the amphibious engineers from Camp Edwards practiced there each day, learning how to land their LCI (landing craft infantry) boats. We didn't know it then, but they were perhaps preparing for a possible invasion of Europe in the coming months of the war.

After a lovely dinner at the Inn (and more stares from the elderly diners), we went up to our rooms to dress for our first night at the USO Club in downtown Falmouth. It was a lovely summer evening, so we enjoyed the fifteen minute walk to town. We were ecstatic when we entered the USO and found hundreds of servicemen: tall handsome engineers from Camp Edwards, Air Force personnel from Otis Air Force Base, and many sailors from nearby ships and installations. We were overwhelmed by the choices and it wasn't long before we were all happily dancing to the latest tunes of the day. When the dance ended, we were escorted back to the Inn by some of the fellows we had been dancing with and each couple selected a secluded spot on the large porch. If it was too bright, our escort unscrewed the overhead light bulb and soon the Inn was in complete darkness. After an hour or so of "necking" and smoking their cigarettes, we said goodnight and promised to meet them the following night at the Club.

We quietly returned to our rooms, chatting about the wonderful evening we had had while some of the girls put their hair up in pin curls with bobby pins. With natural curly hair, I was spared that ordeal and was usually asleep before they finished the nightly task. Shirley had gone to the bathroom and she suddenly burst into the room, foaming at the mouth! We didn't know what to do until someone said she must be having an epileptic siege and we should get her to a hospital. "I'm not having a fit!", she screamed. "I just washed my mouth out with soap and you should all do the same! If you don't you might come down with syphilis or gonorrhea!" Since we didn't know what diseases they were or how you caught them (and of course neither did Shirley), we decided to take our chances rather than go through that ritual every night, but Shirley faithfully did. She did however, break out with a pimple just above her upper lip, and it took some convincing to assure her it wasn't a venereal disease!

By the end of the week, we had broken all of the promises we had made to our mothers, but seemed to be none the worse for it. We returned to the Cape several weekends that summer and Shirley, Flo, and Margie continued relationships they had made during our first visit.

At the end of our first week at the Inn, the General Manager came out to speak with us. He told us he could no longer accept reservations from us because we made too much noise late at night and his guests were complaining. He also found out we were bribing the night clerk to steal crackers and cheese from the kitchen for our midnight snacks! We were crushed because there was no other place as nice for the price, so we would call to make reservations under a fictitious name. It got to be a joke, even with the General Manager who was surprised to see us again and would ask "and what name did you use this time?" Deep down, I think he really liked us and we did try to be less noisy, just to please him.

Enlistment Time

In the Fall of 1942 the Millbury boys began to enlist one by one and there were many farewell parties to see them off. We had a gala party for the first one to go and held it at Zon's Spaghetti House in Sutton, a nearby town. Half the town of Millbury turned out, but he returned from Ft. Devens in Ayer, MA the next day, having been declared 4F. I don't recall why, but many young men were given this classification for reasons we didn't think were too serious. It was a blow to all of them who wanted to join their friends in the various branches of service.

My brother and Buster Ethier, who I was dating at the time, went to enlist in the Marines. Buster was accepted but my brother was turned down because of his bite! I think by the end of the war they were taking fellows with or without teeth!! So my brother enlisted in the Navy and after his basic training was assigned to the Armed Guard Center in Brooklyn, NY. Buster went to a marine base in SC, I believe, for his basic training.

IN FRONT OF DOLAN'S NEWS STAND
FOR THE BOYS

Maurice O'Brien and Bernard Devoe enlisted in the Army Air Corps and went to Florida for their basic training.

Joe Goryl enlisted in the Army and Francis & Johnny Hamilton (cousins) enlisted in the Navy.

Now we were finally without male companionship and felt we would wither and die old maids at an early age. Little did we know how soon we would be back in the arms of men from other parts of the United States! The Navy soon would arrive at Holy Cross College and Worcester Polytechnic Institute, and the Army at Clark University. And we didn't waste any time getting to know many of them, including soldiers who were stationed at Ft. Devens in Ayer, MA.

Since the walls of the camp were mostly devoid of pictures, we decided to ask each serviceman if he could send us a pillow case of the base where he was stationed. This was an easy task since we all wrote often to our friends and relatives in service. Soon we had enough pillow cases to cover every inch of wall space in the camp! They were very colorful and each one was different and they became quite a conversation piece, admired by all who visited our humble abode.

Coconut Grove, Boston

Every year, on the weekend before Thanksgiving, Holy Cross and their number one rival, Boston College, met for the final football game of the year. Since we attended many of the Holy Cross games at Fitton Field in Worcester, we decided to go to Boston for this exciting event in November of 1942. We made reservations at the Statler Hotel for Saturday night, and even had dates lined up for that evening in Boston. A close friend named Bob was in the Navy and stationed in Boston. He had lined up five buddies to take us out on the town. We felt the Coconut Grove would be our choice since it was right next door.

We returned to the hotel after the game and had a message at the reception desk from Bob. He said they were restricted to base for some reason or another and we naturally were extremely disappointed. We went out to dinner and then returned to our rooms. Around 11:00 p.m. we decided to go down to the cocktail lounge for a drink and couldn't believe what we saw in the lobby. Charred and badly burned bodies were lying everywhere and we thought there had been an explosion in the hotel. We were told that there had been a fire at the Coconut Grove nightclub and it was chilling to think that we could have been some of those bodies lying in the hotel and on the sidewalks outside. We immediately tried to call home, but couldn't get through to anyone. We continued to try into the early morning hours, but it wasn't until the next day that we were able to reach our folks who had been frantically trying to reach us. We knew some of the Holy Cross players who died in that horrible fire and felt it was fate that we were still alive.

As a result of this horrible event, fire laws for public places were changed drastically. No more artificial flowers or plants (there were many artificial palm trees in the Coconut Grove) in public nightclubs, and more exits required depending uon the size of the facility. There were only one or two exits out of the Coconut Grove and people were piled up in front of these, trying to exit.

The Army Convoy Disaster

One snowy Saturday in the winter of 1942, we were preparing for a party with some of our friends from Holy Cross. It was going to be at Flo's because she had a large enclosed front porch which had plenty of comfy chairs and room to dance to our favorite Big Band records. We had all the latest Glenn Miller, Tommy Dorsey, Woody Herman recordings and many other popular bands of that era. None of the fellows we knew at the Cross had automobiles so they normally took the bus to Millbury. We found out late in the afternoon that because of the heavy snow predicted, all buses had been cancelled. I still don't understand why Elva's father let us borrow his new hydromatic Oldsmobile to pick the fellows up, but off Elva and I went with me at the wheel. The roads weren't too bad at 7:00 p.m. if you took it easy, which of course we did. I can't remember why Elva asked me to drive, but because the car was new, I was more careful than ever.

When we arrived at the college, only two brave souls were willing to venture forth – Jimmy Scondras and Frank Calabrese. Jimmy got into the front seat with Elva and me, and Frank hopped in the back seat alone. We drove slowly through Quinsigamond Village and then had to cross over a main artery through Worcester – the southwest cutoff. There was a traffic light at this intersection, but it was not working that night, presumably because of the weather. Visibility had worsened since we left home, but I did stop to make sure there was no traffic approaching on the cutoff. As we started across the road, we felt a sudden thump and before we knew it, we were sitting atop a high embankment on the other side of the highway. We all got out and found the entire left back side of the car was badly damaged, but luckily Frank was sitting on the opposite side. Had Jimmy climbed into the back seat with him, one of them would probably have been killed. By this time there were many soldiers descending the embankment to see if we were all right. They helped us down to the highway, and we could now see a long line of Army trucks and vehicles on the roadway. We had run into a convoy!! Our car was so badly damaged we could not drive it, so we again had to make a decision about who to call. We decided it was better to call Flo's father rather than Elva's father, so we went into a diner across the highway, and made the dreaded call. Again Ralph came to our rescue and was not too happy when he surveyed the wrecked Oldsmobile.

The other girls had piled into Ralph's car as they didn't want to miss any of the excitement, but I can still remember being sick to my stomach and regretting that I had agreed to drive that night. While Ralph was giving pertinent information to the officers with the convoy, the girls were busy chatting with the G.I.'s, I just wanted to go home and die.

I think it was months before this incident was settled because of all the red tape involved with the US Army. I'm sure it also took weeks before Elva's Dad got his car back as spare parts were scarce during the war. He was the Chief Chemist at the Felters Co. in Millbury and any time I spotted him walking downtown at lunch time, I would run the other way.

I just found out a couple of years ago from Elva that her Dad didn't realize I had been driving that night! I think to protect me, she just hadn't mentioned it to him, and so he assumed she was at the wheel. That's why we are still close friends after 70 years!

Armed Guard Center, Brooklyn, NY

Having completed his basic training in Newport, RI, my brother was stationed in Brooklyn, NY at the Armed Guard Center. The Navy personnel at this Center manned the guns on the hundreds of Liberty Ships that were carrying cargo to Britain during the war. This was a dangerous mission as German U-boats were sinking these ships at an enormous rate and each time he made a crossing he never knew whether he would return safely.

In June of 1943 we decided to take a weekend trip to New York City to visit him at the Center. In those days, you dressed to the hilt to go anywhere outside of Millbury, and I remember I had bought an expensive new hat with a matching pocketbook. The large brimmed hat had a long feather rising up about eight inches. After getting in and out of several crowded elevators the feather slowly wilted. We took the train from Worcester and because they were so crowded during the War, we sat on our luggage all the way to Manhattan!

We managed to find our way to Brooklyn and finally to

the Center and we were ushered up to the second floor of a very large building. We sat on benches and were told that my brother would be with us shortly. We lit up our Debs' cigarettes and soon had filled the place with smoke. Ray soon appeared with a handsome sailor at his side, and his first remarks were, "Jesus C. – where did you get those hats, and haven't you learned to inhale yet?"

Mortified, if I had a gun I would have shot him. When he finished laughing at us, he introduced us to his friend Dick, who was very shy and extremely handsome and spoke with a southern accent. We visited for an hour or so and then said goodbye. All we could talk about the rest of the weekend was how good looking Dick was and I made sure Ray brought him to Millbury on his next weekend pass.

I don't remember exactly when it happened, but not too many weeks later Dick went to sea on one of the Liberty Ships which was torpedoed and sank in the North Atlantic. He spent 30 days on a raft with some of his shipmates. Some died but he and a couple of others survived and were finally picked up and brought to the Bahamas to recuperate. They were received there by Edward, the former Duke of Edinburgh, and his wife Wallis Simpson. He was given the assignment of Governor of the Bahamas after he abdicated the throne in 1936 to marry Wallis.

Dick never went to sea again and was assigned to a Special Services Group and went on many bond drives with Hollywood stars. Because he was so handsome, he also did a lot of modeling for advertising agencies in the New York City area.

Little did any of us ever imagine at that time that Shirley would marry Dick before the war ended!

The Boys From WPI

Our last full summer at the Hut Sut was in 1942. Elva had just graduated from high school but would not enter Smith College until the Fall, and Flo was still a Junior. Shirl, Phyl, Margaret and I were all working but we would spend every weekend on Lake Singletary and took any vacation time coming to us during those summer months.

G. Georgeopulo, C. Hawarth, B. Hawkins, G. Ferrera

One summer night in 1943 Shirl, Flo, Phyl, and I were having a snack at a restaurant in Worcester which was near the Capitol Theater where we had just seen a movie. There were two sailors having a drink at the bar and they were trying to get our attention We smiled at them and they approached our table and introduced themselves as new V-12 Naval recruits at Worcester Polytechnic Institute. They had previously been students at Lafayette College in Pennsylvania and had joined the V-12 Naval Program and were eventually sent to WPI to complete their military obligations and their education. This was a lucky break for them as none of them went to sea until the war had ended.

We told them about our camp on Lake Singletary and they said they would love to visit us. We invited them to visit the following weekend and asked if they could bring four more sailors as there were six of us. They said that would not be a problem as they could probably bring the entire student body if we desired!

We told them which bus to take from Worcester to Millbury which was the only one that would go as far as Lake Singletary. We said we would meet them at Singletary Nook which was a very short walk from our camp.

They arrived on the 2 o'clock bus and couldn't wait to get into their bathing trunks when we got to the camp. There were the two we had met in Worcester, Ludlow Kaeser and Adam Shaner and they introduced us to Mel Bredahl, George Ferrera, Pete Tartaglio and Cooly Howarth. They were all extremely good looking and we knew we were in for a weekend of fun.

Elva had brought the sailboat down from her family's camp nearby and the boys were ecstatic when they saw it, especially Lud who said he had a sailboat at his home in New Haven, CT. Knowing that at least one of them knew how to handle a sailboat, Elva agreed to let them go out alone for a sail across the lake.

They had each brought a duffle bag with them and placed them in the bedrooms. Shirl, our CIA agent, decided again that we should go through their bags. We really protested this time because we didn't want to find condoms again which would ruin a perfectly wonderful weekend. Shirl insisted it was better to find out now than later so we gave in and opened each bag. We didn't find condoms, but in each bag was a fifth of liquor and in our eyes that was almost as bad. We did start drinking a little after our vacation on the Cape, but since they had brought so much liquor, we felt sure they would get quite drunk after we left for home that night. And since they all smoked, they could possibly burn the camp down. Shirl convinced us we had to get rid of the booze before they returned from their sail, so we brought all six fifths to the kitchen While Shirl proudly manned the hand pump, we opened each bottle and poured it down the sink. We then returned the duffle bags to the bedrooms we had snatched them from.

When the boys returned from their sail we all went for a dip in the lake and then began to prepare dinner. We were happy they didn't look in their duffle bags before we left for home that night and we had a wonderful time singing and dancing.

We returned to the camp early the next morning to prepare their breakfast, and, of course, we were met by six very unhappy sailors!! They asked what we did with their liquor, and when we told them, they went ballistic! At best they thought we had just hidden the bottles, but when they learned the truth they prepared to leave. We begged them not to go and apologized profusely. They were not too happy with our reasons for getting rid of it and told us they had spent precious money from their meager monthly allowance to buy the liquor.

For some reason, perhaps the lure of the lake and the sailboat and canoe outside (and maybe perhaps the food and our company) they decided to stay for the rest of the weekend. We truly had a wonderful time and loved each one of them. So we invited them back the next weekend, assuring them they could bring liquor only if they promised to share it with us!

George played on the WPI varsity football team so in the Fall we went to many of the home games to cheer for him. He was one of their best players and a wonderful guy, and we all loved him dearly.

The WPI boys came back many weekends in the summer of 1943-44 and soon Mel began to date Flo and Shirl went out with George until she met Dick. They brought many other fellows to the Hut Sut but I can't remember all of their names - Ed Polk, Earl Balkom, Jim Johnson, Charlie Brace, Bob Hawkins, Ed Sheehy, Matt Tirrell, Bob Meyer, Bob Gamble, Alvin Twing, Paul Marshall, K. Miles and Lionel Brooks, to name a few (from our Guest Book which I hold most dear).

And best of all, we loved their motto: Victory in 12 Years or We'll Fight!!

A Dreaded Telegram From The War Department

One night in late February, 1944, I had a phone call from Dev's mother, Ann Devoe, whom I had never met, and wondered why she was calling me. She began to cry and told me they had just received word that Dev was missing in action. I was so stunned I could hardly speak and told her I would be right down to see her and Dev's father, Hector. I called the other girls and broke the bad news. We all went down to Dev's home on Millbury Avenue. Needless to say, it was a very sad evening for all of us but it was the first of many trips we made to visit and console them and we became fast friends. We exchanged pictures of Dev and I think our visits did help to keep their spirits up. I had received my last letter from Dev sometime in January and it was written on New Year's Eve, 1943. It was longer than usual and he said he didn't know why he had rambled on as he normally only wrote one page. That got my hopes up and I immediately responded to him. It took a while for mail to reach servicemen and for theirs to reach people at home, as all mail was censored. I didn't expect to hear from him for some time.

Ann had heard from the wives of the pilot and co-pilot of their B17 Flying Fortress, as well as some of the relatives of other crew members. The 15th Air Force was stationed in Foggia, Italy, and they were returning back to their base from a daylight bombing mission against German industrial targets in Regensberg, Germany on Feb. 22, 1944. They had been heavily riddled with flack, but hoped to make it back to their base. But luck was not with them and they went down in the Adriatic Sea. We all waited and prayed that Dev had survived, but after what seemed like an eternity, they were all declared dead. A funeral mass was held for Dev at St. Bridget's Church in Millbury and half the town turned out to honor him.

He was a tail gunner on the B-17 and when he would come home on leave before he left the states, he would jokingly tell us that after each bombing mission they would have to replace the tail gunner who was a sitting duck in the tail of the plane. He had completed 14 missions over enemy territory so he still had 11 to go. When he completed gunnery school in Florida they wanted him to stay on as an instructor, but he wanted to see action along with his buddies who had joined the Army, Navy, and Marines.

I was devastated for a long time as I had never told the other girls that I was in love with him. I knew he was going with someone from East Millbury, but I guess I never gave up hope. He knew I was going out with Buster in 1942 and I knew he would never ask me out because of that. Decent guys didn't cut in on other girls' boyfriends. I had told him in my last letter to him that I didn't want to hurt Buster by breaking up just as he was going into service, but I was never in love with him. Of course that letter never reached him and eventually was returned to me..

Ann gave me a beautiful photograph of Dev which he had taken on his last leave home. I still have that picture and the colors have not faded, nor have the memories of my first love - a sweet, handsome guy who died all too young. He was a Staff Sgt. and was so proud of his wings and the stripes on his uniform and we all were so proud of him.

When I was living in Florida in the late eighties, I went to an Air Show of vintage WWII planes and one of them on display was a B-17. Visitors were allowed into the planes and I had to stoop as I maneuvered my way through the narrow aisle to the tail gunner's turret at the back of the aircraft. Dev was over 6 feet tall and how cramped he must have been, sitting in that small area, always knowing that death was just a few direct hits away. I somehow felt close to him again in that aircraft.

The Final Days Of World War II

We closely followed D-Day on June 6, 1944 when the Allied forces landed on the beaches of Normandy in France. We didn't know any of the fellows who were involved in that operation, but we did know that Buster Ethier and Jimmy Scondras (from Holy Cross) were both involved in many bloody battles in the South Pacific, including Iwo Jima, Saipan, and Tinian. Jimmy was killed on Iwo Jima but luckily Buster survived all of these battles and returned home when the war ended.

We celebrated VE Day on May 8, 1945 when the Axis surrendered in Berlin, Germany. and VJ Day on August 14, 1945 when the Japanese surrendered.

Dingle Tower

In the summer of 1947, Flo's folks (mother, father, and grandfather) decided they would like to spend one last vacation with Flo who was to be married in October of that year. Her mother, Susie, had close friends in Halifax, Nova Scotia, so they planned to drive to Halifax and spend a week there. Flo asked me if I would like to join them and I happily said yes since I have never been to Nova Scotia.

It was a long but most interesting ride through New Brunswick, Canada where we stayed overnight in St. John, and then on to Moncton and the Bay of Fundy where we witnessed the phenomenon of the reverse tide. The tides are so strong you can watch the Petitcodiac River swell and reverse directions. You can also sit in your car on Magnetic Hill and watch as you mysteriously coast uphill!! We finally arrived in Halifax, weary and ready for a good night's sleep at the Canadian National Hotel, probably the largest and best hotel in the city.

The folks planned to sleep late the next morning and then Susie was going to set up visits with old friends in the area, so Flo and I planned to explore the city and its highlights.

We were driving along behind a local bus when we noticed a handsome young man flagging the bus to stop. Before he entered the bus he gave us a big smile and a little wave, so we decided to follow the bus. We went a few miles out of town and finally the bus pulled over to make a stop. Out stepped the young man who now motioned for us to wait and as I was driving, Flo rolled down the window to talk to him. He said he had noticed our Massachusetts license plate and said he had some free time and would be happy to show us the sights if this was our first visit to Halifax. We told him it was our first time in the city so he jumped in next to Flo, introduced himself (a fine Irish name) and threw his hat and overcoat into the back seat, displaying wavy black hair and a wonderful Irish smile, and the white collar of a Roman Catholic priest!!

Flo and I exchanged glances that said we couldn't believe we had picked up a Catholic priest, but we were not about to let it spoil our day. Since we were both Protestant, we didn't have to go to confession – that was his problem! He told us what turns to make which would take us to Dingle Tower on the outskirts of town. We were not too impressed with Dingle Tower, but we found picnic tables around the tower so we sat and talked for quite a while. He told us how long he had been in Halifax, where his church was, and that he was a Jesuit priest and still had time to get out of the priesthood if he decided it was not for him.

Then he suggested we take a look from the top of the tower and since it was so narrow, that we should go up with him one at a time. I told Flo to go first and I walked around the grounds, waiting for them to come down. I happened to glance up after 10 minutes and found him kissing her! To say I was shocked was putting it mildly. What was she thinking of with her wedding date just three weeks away!

They finally came down and now it was my turn. The same thing happened and although I was still in shock, I must say I enjoyed it – after all, I had never kissed a priest before and I had no commitments at the time.

We finally left and dropped him off at the same street corner where we had picked him up and he asked if we were free to meet him again the next day at the same time. We told him we could but had to come up with a good excuse to again get the car the following afternoon. This happened again on the next three days and finally Flo's mother, Susie, wanted to know where we were going each afternoon. We had to lie to her but weren't sure she was accepting our excuses. Saturday rolled around and Susie said they were going to use the car to visit friends just outside of Halifax, so we had lunch with them at the hotel and then just sat in the lobby for a while. Suddenly a group of priests walked by and sure enough, there was our Irish priest smiling at us. Susie caught the exchange of glances and wanted to know why he was smiling at us. We said we had no idea, but I think she began to put two and two together although she never questioned us further.

When we told him on Friday that we couldn't get the car on Saturday, he asked us to attend his church on Sunday where he would be officiating. It was a real struggle to get the car on Sunday, but since it was our last day in Halifax, Flo's folks agreed and said they would attend a Protestant church nearby. So off we went to mass and said our goodbyes to our new friend after the service. He said if he stayed in the priesthood he might be transferred to Pomfret, Ct. and would look us up. But we never heard from him again. We did ask him on one of those jaunts to Dingle Tower if it was a sin for him to be meeting two Protestant girls like this. He said he had a cousin who was also a Jesuit priest and they heard each other's confessions each week! If we'd had more time in Halifax, I'm sure we would have been double dating!!

Several years later I was working in a small insurance office in Newtown, CT and at lunchtime I would tell the girls about some of my wilder experiences before I was married. They loved the Dingle Tower story and one of the girls said she had a friend in Pomfret and would try to find out if our Halifax friend had ever been assigned to the Catholic church there. She inquired and found out he never came to Pomfret, but his younger brother (who was also a priest) had moved to their parish. She said he, too, was very handsome and every girl in town was in love with him!

All Good Things Must Come To An End

We knew someone eventually would buy the precious land occupied by the Hut Sut. Some years later when I drove up to Lake Singletary to take a look at it, in its place was a lovely new home. I was very sad as I wanted it to be there forever. I sat for a long time reminiscing about our wonderful days on Lake Singletary.

Shirley was the first to marry in the Fall of 1945 when she and Dick McLaughlin wed and moved to Houston, TX.

Elva was married in June of 1946, right after she graduated from Smith College. She married George Carpenter who was a handsome Lt. in the Army Air Corps. They settled down in New York where George was an interior decorator at Macy's.

Flo married Mel Bredahl in October of 1947 and they settled down in Philadelphia, PA .

Phyl married Charles Morgan in the Fall of 1949 and they settled down in Chepachet, RI, where Charlie was a salesman for Metropolitan Life.

I was the last one to marry, and wed Bruce Cambridge in August of 1950, and we settled down in North Haven, CT. Bruce was a Sales Engineer with Drew Chemical Co.

Margaret never married and we lost contact with her over the years since our Hut Sut days. We tried to include her in some of our get-togethers, but she chose not to be part of our group anymore. We missed her but I think possibly it was because she never married.

Marriage Did Not End Our Relationship

After we all married most of us moved to different parts of the country. Bruce and I moved to Blackstone Virginia immediately after our marriage when he was assigned to Camp Pickett, VA. Our honeymoon was brief when his unit, the 118th Medical Battalion, was sent to Munich, Germany. I joined him there a few months later and it was a wonderful year and a half. When he was discharged we returned to our new home in North Haven, CT.

Shirley and Dick lived in Houston, TX for a few years and then moved to Manchester, NH where Dick had a job with Seagrams promoting a new brand of Bourbon.

Flo & Mel moved to Philadelphia after their marriage and later spent a couple of years in MN before finally settling down in CT where Mel started his own chain business.

Phyl & Charlie moved to Chepachet, CT after their marriage, later moved back to Millbury for a short while,

80

and then settled down in Norwell, MA when Charlie became a General Manager for Metropolitan Life Insurance Co.

Elva and George moved to New York City after their marriage where George worked for Macy's as an Interior Decorator. They moved to NH in 1950 where George started his own business, selling furniture and continuing his career as an interior decorator.

When we all moved back to New England, we began to see more of each other and got together at least three or four times a year. We became very friendly with Margie (Banks) and Maurice Roberts who lived in West Millbury and had a lovely camp on Lake Singletary. We had wonderful summer weekends at their camp and in the winter we would get together at Shirl & Dick's home in Manchester for ski weekends. None of us were very good skiers but we still bravely attempted the slopes at the popular ski resorts in that area.

Bruce and I always had Fall weekends at our home in CT and would attend football games at Yale University. Bruce would bring litters home from the Medical Battalion (he stayed in the Guards to complete his 20 years of service) and they were spread all over the living room floor for the fellows to sleep on.

BACK ROW: *CHARLIE, FLO, MEL*
FRONT ROW: *DICK, SHIRL, BEV, PHYL, ELVA, GEORGE*

We had many wonderful weekends at Flo & Mel's summer home on Lake Winnipesaukee in Laconia, NH. Flo & Mel had kept in contact with George Ferrera over the years, and he and his wife joined us for some of those reunions. It was always great to see George again after all those years.

Elva & George didn't join us until later years when their business was established enough for George to get away for a weekend. But we would see them on our ski weekends at Shirl & Dick's because they were close by in Rye, NH.

Losing Our Loved Ones

Bruce was the first to die in October of 1973. Dick died in September of 1993, and Mel passed away in 1996. Shirl died in 2003 and Flo in 2004.

Although Shirl & Dick and Flo & Mel were gone, Elva & George and I still see Phyl & Charlie frequently. We drive to Norwell to have lunch with them, or they occasionally come up to NH. We are constantly in touch by telephone.

The Millennium Reunion

As New Year's Eve approached in 1999, Elva & George invited Phyl & Charlie, Shirl, Flo and me to their lovely home in Rye, NH for the weekend to celebrate the Millennium. It was a wonderful weekend and we indulged in gourmet food and drinks and much expensive champagne. We did a lot of reminiscing and missed the presence of Dick, Mel & Bruce even more, but it was a joyous and special weekend for all of us.

It was the last weekend the five of us would be together.

The Last Hurrah At The Hut Sut

Bruce and I returned from his assignment with the CT National Guard in the Spring of 1953 and we were warmly welcomed back by all of our friends.

Since the Hut Sut was still intact and fully furnished, we decided to have one final farewell party there. Everyone was available except Elva & George: Flo & Mel, Phyl & Charlie, Shirl & Dick, Margie & Maurice, and Eva & Arnold Higginson who were also our close friends from Auburn, MA (born & raised in Millbury).

Bruce and I wore our German outfits – lederhosen & Alpine jacket for Bruce, and a dirndl dress and Alpine hat for me. I think we even attempted a schuplatz dance after a few drinks!

It was a very merry evening, with lots of laughs and reminiscing. Our pillow cases were still adorning the walls of the camp and nothing had really changed so it was easy to get caught up in all the wonderful memories we shared of that place and time.

Our Final Days In Dubrovnik

After reminiscing about my WWII days, I returned to our hotel room. Bruce was awake but complained of pain in one of his shoulders so I called the front desk to see if they could call a Dr. to come to the hotel. One arrived that afternoon but she didn't speak English. She prescribed some medication which didn't do much good, and I prayed Bruce would be all right until we reached London the next day.

It was not a pleasant flight as Bruce was now so weak he was unable to carry any of our luggage. I prayed and prayed he would make it to London. As soon as we arrived at the Cumberland Hotel in London I called the Front Desk and they contacted a Dr. who came within an hour. His name was Dr. Ismay and he examined Bruce and told me he was a very sick man. I told him we were flying to the states the next day and he told me that would be risky in his present condition. So he arranged to admit him to the London Clinic where he went immediately.

Dr. Ismay consulted with Bruce's Dr. in Waterbury, CT, to

get a history of his illnesses, and then brought in a local surgeon, Mr. Shand, to assess his problems. Surgeons are addressed as Mr. and not Dr. in London, or at least they were at that time. They both decided he had gangrene in his system as his stomach was quite distended. They took out gallons of the poison and then decided to do exploratory surgery. Because of his history of pancreatitis, they suspected an abscess might have formed where the pancreas had been, so on Sunday night, October 17, they operated on him.

I had spent most of the six days and evenings at his bedside prior to the operation and hadn't had much sleep. But the night after he was operated on, the nurse told me I should return to the hotel for a good night's sleep, as she felt the worse was over.

I was staying at the Londoner Hotel and the only interesting part of this frightening ordeal was the fifteen minute walk to the London Clinic. I had to walk down Baker Street which was made famous by Sherlock Holmes, and also had to cross Wimpole Street, made famous by the Barretts of Wimpole Street.

I returned to the hotel and had dinner and went to my room and immediately fell into a deep sleep when I hit the bed. I was awakened with a ringing sound and finally realized it was the telephone. I picked it up and heard, "Mrs. Cambridge, this is Mr. Shand. Your husband has just died". When his words sunk in, I replied "How could he just die? - no one just dies!" He told me his condition worsened as the evening wore on and he was having trouble breathing. They gave him oxygen to no avail and he died at approximately one o'clock. It was now 1:15 a.m.

I must have gone into shock as I felt very cold and began to shiver. I piled on the blankets from the other twin bed, but could not warm up. I had some gin and some sleeping tablets the Dr. had given me, so I took those. I knew I had to call someone back in the states so I called the man I worked for, Hamilton Leach, and told him Bruce had just died. He was shocked but said he would get someone from the office to come to London to be with me as soon as it could be arranged. Luckily it was one of my best friends, Eve Romaine. who had a passport and she arrived the next afternoon. I also called one of my friends in Heritage Village where we lived in Southbury, CT, and gave her the sad news.

Mr. Shand asked me if I would be able t come to his office the next morning and I said I would. But I never awakened until I heard one of the maids open the door to my room and there stood Mr. Shand and Dr. Ismay. They were concerned when I never showed up so came to see if I was all right. I couldn't believe they had taken the time to come to my hotel to check on me.

Eve arrived shortly after that and was a Godsend. She picked out a casket to carry Bruce home and went to the American Embassy to make arrangements for his body to be flown back to CT.

We weren't leaving for the states until the next day. Eve had never been to London and I was so grateful for her arrival I suggested a bus tour of London so she could at least see some of the sights. So we sat on the upper open deck and at least she got a "bird's eye view" of some of the outstanding and historic landmarks in London.

We arrived in Southbury, CT on Saturday afternoon and I couldn't believe how many old friends were there to greet me. In addition to my brother and sister-in-law, all of the Bramanville Girls and their husbands, plus many more friends from Millbury and North Haven, CT, plus one friend from NJ.

I was devastated by my loss, but friends consoled me and kept me busy. I returned to work after three weeks, and it was the best therapy I could have received. I also finally started playing tennis and a friend and I went to a Tennis School at Choate School in Waterbury, CT the next summer and I became engrossed in the game. We had tennis courts in the complex where I had a condo, and we played every night after dinner. This was also good therapy for me because I didn't get home until 7:30 or 8 o'clock, past the time Bruce used to arrive from his job in Bedford, NY. I used to listen for his car pulling into the garage under our Carriage House.

I have wanted to write this book about the Bramanville Girls for many years and finally I have put it all down on paper. I am now 86 but my memory of those wonderful days is still clear and intact, and I'm only sorry that Shirl and Flo will never get to read it, especially Shirl who made so many episodes funny and memorable. I shall dedicate the book to her.

Back Row: Shirl, Phyl; Front Row: Flo, Elva, Betty, Bev

As I look back over those wonderful Hut Sut days, I can't help but think had we officially been part of the USO, we would have been known as the Hut Sut Canteen!! Although we could not be compared to the Stage Door Canteen, we certainly did our share to entertain men from all the services during the years 1941 though 1945. And, of course, we had one helluva time doing it!!

CPSIA information can be obtained at www.ICGtesting.com
Printed in the USA
241996LV00001B/50/P